the BLUEFIN BONANZA

lifting the lid on the lucrative trade in one of the most endangered species on the planet

A BOOK BY

Anieszka Banks
Benjamin Baldwin
Katja Dylla
Helena Fletcher
Josefin Robertsson
Emily Wilson
Wietse van der Werf

Editor: Rose Newell

CONTENTS

Fisherman's friend?	8	Index	70
Thunnus Thynnus	14	Glossary	73
Fishing for trouble	24	Acknowledgements	80
Farming fishes	40	Photo credits	82
Fishy business	48		
Time for action	60		

CHAPTER ONE

FISHERMAN'S FRIEND?

It is a warm summer evening in Sète, a busy harbour town in Southern France. François Bertet, the skipper of a fishing vessel called the Recife, steps into the wheelhouse. He checks a couple of gauges on the dashboard in front of him and turns the ignition key: with a strong shudder, the engines stop and the 33-metre-long fishing boat grinds to a halt. François lifts a book out of a drawer and notes down some final details of today's trip. Shutting the book, he closes the drawer and switches off the wheelhouse light. He steps outside and shuts the hatch, thus locking the steel beast. Another day of honest work has come to an end. The rest of the crew are walking down the pier. Our skipper follows. A couple of beers and then straight to bed. He needs rest for an early rise the next morning and another long day at sea.

François is an industrial fisherman, his catch is usually bluefin tuna – an expensive fish. What he represents is nothing like the romantic picture which is so often painted: the lone fisherman, out at sea for days on end, battling the elements to catch a few little fish to feed his family, who are all the while eagerly awaiting his return to shore. François belongs to a new generation of fishermen. A generation which will stop at nothing

to catch everything that can be eaten in the sea. Moreover, he targets the increasingly endangered bluefin tuna. The lucrative trade in this endangered fish is among the most destructive and immoral industries in the world.

The oceans are the greatest wilderness we share on this planet. All the seas, lakes, rivers, streams, wetlands and creeks amount to ninety-nine percent of all space on the planet which supports life. The oceans were once abundant with life but over the last few decades relentless industrial fishing has decimated ocean life to such an extent that we are now headed for environmental disaster, impossible for ocean life to recover from. The latest figures show a bleak picture: unless something radically changes in the way humans exploit the seas, all large fish will have disappeared from the oceans within fifty years.

The most immediate crisis we know of is that of the bluefin tuna. The bluefin is one of the most advanced predators on earth. They are the world's largest living bony fish and, after the sailfish, one of the fastest hunters to roam the great seas. In recent years, the species has been so heavily overfished that it is estimated its breeding population may disappear from the Mediterranean Sea within

"ALL THE SEAS, LAKES, RIVERS, STREAMS, WETLANDS AND CREEKS AMOUNT TO NINETY-NINE PERCENT OF ALL SPACE ON THE PLANET WHICH SUPPORTS LIFE."

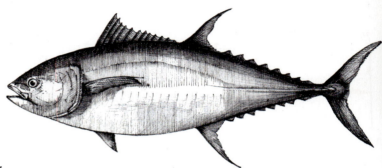

the next five years. Just a handful of corporations, looking to make quick money from the increased prices for this heavily endangered animal, are responsible for pushing it further towards the brink of extinction.

Just imagine for a moment what would happen if a group of people arrived with bulldozers and decided to start cutting down trees everywhere, grinding them up and exporting them to Asia to make paper. Imagine then, for a moment, that the whole operation is heavily subsidised by the European Union, even though it is clear that all the trees in Europe are now endangered and that, once gone,

they will never return. All types and sizes of trees are removed from common land, protected areas, parks, gardens: everything, from everywhere. Small trees are cut down before they have a chance to grow. In some cases the loggers defend their illegal operations with violence and threats, but mostly they operate at night and out of sight, cutting down entire woodlands in a single operation. Would a situation like this be tolerated? Doubtful. There would be a huge movement of people stopping the massacre. People would take direct action. Politicians would not get away with ignoring the issue and the mainstream environmental organisations would at least be able to negotiate the sparing of some trees, in exchange for not opposing the logging of many others. That would at least be something. Unfortunately, the bluefin tuna does not even seem to have that something. The illegal overfishing of bluefin tuna is on the increase and only a handful of people are actively opposing it. How is it possible that despite all the international rules and regulations in place, fishermen can continue their illegal and destructive activities? Is anyone enforcing the law? Who is supposed to take responsibility? And why exactly does the European Union continue to hand out trade subsidies to companies and vessels which catch and process the endangered bluefin tuna?

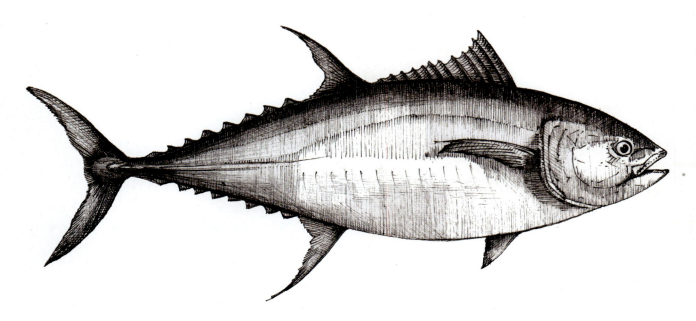

This book uses clear language to describe the race for the last bluefin, which is currently under way in the Mediterranean Sea. It will show you what an amazingly sophisticated animal the bluefin is, what illegal fishing activities are still taking place at sea, and the incredible apathy and unwillingness in the political environment to properly deal with these problems and give the bluefin the protection it so desperately needs.

> "HOW IS IT POSSIBLE THAT DESPITE ALL THE INTERNATIONAL RULES AND REGULATIONS IN PLACE, FISHERMEN CAN CONTINUE THEIR ILLEGAL AND DESTRUCTIVE ACTIVITIES?"

This book is also the starting point of The Black Fish campaign to protect this heavily endangered fish. It is not our intention to simply sit back and write about problems; where possible, we will act to protect and save animals directly. We aim to make a difference: to save the threatened creatures of the sea and make sure that the 'bluefin bonanza' enjoyed by the few corporations making a killing through the demise of the bluefin tuna will be renowned the world over. We hope that reading this book inspires you to join the growing movement of people that oppose the atrocities and are willing to join in and take action. Our readiness to act now will be the only chance this species has of survival.

"IT IS NOT OUR INTENTION TO SIMPLY SIT BACK AND WRITE ABOUT PROBLEMS; WHERE POSSIBLE, WE WILL ACT TO PROTECT AND SAVE ANIMALS DIRECTLY."

CHAPTER TWO

THUNNUS THYNNUS

When thinking of tuna, many people might imagine a piece of dark-red meat on a sushi roll, or a tinned salad ingredient. Industrial fishermen in the Mediterranean might not think of the bluefin tuna in their nets as a pinnacle of evolution that plays an important part in the ocean's ecosystem, but rather of the money to be made from them once fattened in pens and slaughtered. The once common Atlantic Bluefin tuna (Thunnus Thynnus) is on an express train to extinction due to human greed, fuelled by the high demand for bluefin meat on the Japanese sushi and sashimi markets. It is somewhat limiting to confine our view of the magnificent wild bluefin to a prized piece of meat waiting to be harvested. This gross misrepresentation of a remarkable creature does neither their existence nor our capacity for perception justice.

"THE ATLANTIC BLUEFIN IS THE BIGGEST OF THE TUNA SPECIES AND CAN GROW TO GIGANTIC PROPORTIONS."

WHAT'S SO SPECIAL ABOUT BLUEFINS?

Considering the phenomenal variation in size, shape and striking colourations of all the inhabitants of the ocean and its depths, the subtle beauty of the sleek bluefin may have some difficulty in capturing our attention. It might not come across as a very spectacular fish at first glance, but in the case of the tuna fish, looks truly are deceiving. There are eight tuna species in the Thunnus genus, the group of species to which the three species of bluefin tuna belong.

The Atlantic bluefin is the biggest of the tuna species and can grow to gigantic proportions; the biggest one ever caught weighed 679 kg (1,496 lbs). It was caught off Nova Scotia in 1979. Unfortunately, the bluefins have been increasingly exploited since the 1960s and it would be very rare to come across such a giant bluefin nowadays.

Big or small, it is hard not to admire the bluefin for its many characteristics (external and internal) that make it so well adapted to its pelagic, "open sea", habitat. Even its scales are designed to help the animal cut through the surrounding water with little effort; a few beats of the tailfin sets the bluefin off at speeds of up to 90 km/h (55 mph). Its tiny scales mean the bluefin has smooth, nearly frictionless skin, and unlike many other species of fish, the eyes do not protrude but instead lie flat against the head to create a perfect streamline. Just like many deepwater sharks, the bluefin also has a third eye, called the pineal organ, on the top of its head. Light is transferred through the tissues in the pineal window down into the pineal organ, letting the fish know the strength of the light shining down from above,

even if it is as faint as moonlight. It is believed that this may, among other things, help the animals control their vertical movements.

Sometimes the streamlined bluefin benefits from an additional reduction in drag, perhaps to escape predators or to catch prey. Small bluefins have to watch out for every predator big enough to grab them, while the larger individuals are safe from most other species, except for killer whales, mako sharks and, of course, humans. To gain the reduction in drag they can fold back their pectoral fins, which are normally used for steering, into slots along their sides, with the first dorsal fin completely folding down into another slot on the back. The lunate, rigid tailfin is something the bluefin share with all their fellow species in the Scombrid (mackerel) family and the Istiophorid (sailfish and marlin) family. Together with the fastest swimming sharks (those of the Lamnidae family: the great white, the short and longfin mako, the salmon shark and the porbeagle), the tuna and the billfish have evolved a method of swimming that is unique to them: thunniform swimming. According to Richard Ellis in his book *'Tuna: Love, Death, and Mercury'*, this effective method of swimming has evolved independently in each of these groups. This means that, unlike most other species of fish, the bullet-shaped body of the bluefin tuna remains both straight and rigid when in the swimming motion - and their tail is the only part that moves. Meanwhile, its powerful, specially-adapted muscles create horizontal movement in the narrow caudal peduncle, which in turn creates propulsion through the tailfin. The tailfin is always proportional to the bluefin's body size.

There have been several attempts to build robots that mimic the unique efficiency of tuna. Scientists have yet to succeed. We still do not even know the purpose of all the features of the bluefin's exterior, for example the two rows of finlets in front of the tailfin are assumed to contribute to speed but this has not been proven. Equally amazing, however, are the internal characteristics. First of all, the bluefin – paradoxically for a fish – is regionally endothermic (warm-blooded). This enables the fish to survive in waters of considerably different temperatures. Their body temperature remains fairly constant at around 25°C (77°F), while the temperature of their habitats range from 3 to 31°C (37 to 88°F). Remarkably, the bluefins can regulate the temperature in different parts of their body independently of one another, as well as independently of the ambient water temperature, and, for example, raise the temperature of their stomach to speed up metabolism when food is plentiful.

When diving, they can be exposed to temperature fluctuations of 10 to 15°C (50 to 59°F) within a matter of minutes, something that most cold-blooded fish could not withstand. However, it seems that the bigger bluefins are better at maintaining body temperature in colder waters, while the smaller ones need to return frequently to the warmer surface waters and so cannot stay in the cold deep for very long.

This "endothermicity", or the ability to regulate their own body temperature, has enabled the bluefin tuna to move between foraging grounds and also to expand their habitat vertically - they can dive down to depths of at least one thousand metres. Furthermore, the warm muscles provide an extra efficiency boost that makes them formidable hunters. The endothermicity is another trait that they share with billfishes and lamnid sharks, as well as a small number of other fish.

METABOLISM MAGIC

Bluefins warm their eyes, brain, muscles and insides by conserving the heat produced by their metabolism. A net of blood vessels called the rete mirabile (Latin for 'wonderful net') functions as a vascular counter-current heat exchange system, spreading the heat to other tissues. This means that veins containing warm blood that is low in oxygen and arteries with cold blood that has been replenished with oxygen from the gills pass alongside one another, enabling the transfer of heat from the warm venereal blood flowing towards the gills to the arteries with blood flowing back into the body.

"BLUEFINS MUST MOVE FORWARD AT LEAST ONE FULL BODY LENGTH PER SECOND OR DIE FROM OXYGEN DEFICIENCY."

In this way, almost all of the heat in the bloodstream is conserved within the body, as the blood in the veins is already cooled down to within a degree of water temperature by the arterial blood before it reaches the gills. Bluefins need lots of oxygen to maintain their body temperature, high metabolism, stamina and high-speed sprinting abilities. They have a huge gill surface where the oxygen is absorbed from the water into the bloodstream which is up to thirty times larger than that of other fish species. Their hearts are also very large and they have high blood pressure and a fast heart rate.

Bluefins have a lot of blood with a high oxygen capacity. On top of this, they can store a lot of oxygen in their muscles in a protein called myoglobin, which is the reason their flesh has a rich red colour. This oxygen is released during extended muscle activity and helps the bluefin keep the oxygen in their muscles at a fairly steady level, avoiding or delaying the formation of lactic acid, which builds up in muscles running low on oxygen. Diving mammals such as seals and whales have even higher levels of myoglobin to support them during their dives.

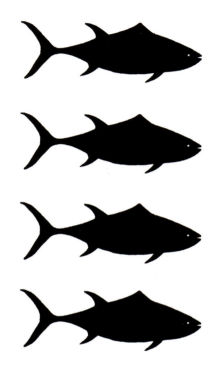

"THE BLUEFIN CAN REGULATE THE
TEMPERATURE IN DIFFERENT PARTS OF ITS
BODY INDEPENDENTLY
OF ONE ANOTHER."

Just like most sharks, the bluefin and other tuna species must constantly move forward to oxygenate themselves, since the gills do not pump water. Instead, water is passed over the gills whilst the tuna swim with their mouths open – this is called 'ramjet breathing'. They must move forward at least one full body length per second or die from oxygen deficiency. Hence, tuna held captive in farms swim in endless circles along the walls of their submerged cages.

The juvenile bluefin, in particular, cross the Atlantic to enjoy the various feeding grounds, primarily located off the coast of North America, where they sometimes stay for several years before heading back as mature fish to one of their known spawning grounds in the Gulf of Mexico or the Mediterranean Sea. Each fish returns to the spot where he or she was born – a phenomenon known as 'spawning site fidelity'. The International Commission for the Conservation of Atlantic Tunas (ICCAT), which has been put in charge of managing the bluefin tuna fishing industry, is currently treating the tuna in the east and west Atlantic as two different populations divided by the 45°W meridian, where the crossing between stocks is considered more or less insignificant to the fisheries management issue. This represents a potential threat to the species since the juveniles and adolescents cross the Atlantic on a regular basis. Adult bluefins also cross the ocean, although it is not known to what extent.

> "IN LESS THAN 40 DAYS THE BLUEFINS CAN TRAVEL THE LENGTH OF THEIR VAST HABITAT FROM THE NORTH ATLANTIC OCEAN TO THE MEDITERRANEAN SEA"

A BLUEFIN LIFESTYLE

In less than 40 days the bluefins can – and do – travel the length of their vast habitat of the North Atlantic Ocean and its adjacent areas, such as the Mediterranean Sea and the Gulf of Mexico. Not only are the bluefin fast, they also have amazing stamina which allows them to undertake this journey sometimes several times a year. They normally travel in schools of up to 40 individuals, but a school can be much larger and is always made up of fish of the same size, even though there may be a mix of different tuna species.

Bluefins are opportunistic and feed on a range of different prey; invertebrates such as jellyfish and salp, sponges, crabs, squid and many different species of fish. They eat more or less anything they come across that is of a size they can handle, but adults prefer to feed on fish – in the Mediterranean, anchovy is a favourite – while the juveniles would not pass up on some crustaceans and cephalopods.

THE MEDITERRANEAN SEA

The East Atlantic population that spawns in the Mediterranean is believed to reach maturity at 4-5 years of age, at a size of 110 – 120 cm (approx. 3.5 to 4 feet) and 30-35 kg (approx. 66 to 77 lbs). The older the fish is, the more eggs she will produce; a female of 15-20 years can carry up to 45 million eggs, whereas a five year old female produces an average of five million. The chance of a bluefin egg growing into an adult fish is 1 in 40 million, which means that it takes eight female first-spawners to produce one single offspring that will live to see adulthood.

"A FULLY GROWN FEMALE BLUEFIN CAN CARRY UP TO 45 MILLION EGGS IN ONE SPAWNING CYCLE."

In the Mediterranean Sea, spawning occurs between May and August, but the peak of the spawning season is June to July. The bluefin spawn near the surface in the early hours before sunrise, where water temperatures are close to 24°C (75°F) and salinity and currents are optimal to ensure the larvae have plankton to feed on. It is unclear whether the mature tuna spawn every year or every two to three years. The individuals in the eastern population – if they do not end up in a fishing net – are known to live for up to 20 years, whereas their close relatives in the western population are estimated to live for at least 32 years.

As you can see, the bluefin tuna is one of a kind. What makes its continued exploitation and possible extinction especially alarming is the fact that this incredibly advanced and sophisticated animal, shaped by a millennia of evolution, is now on course to be fished to extinction within our lifetimes.

CHAPTER THREE

FISHING FOR TROUBLE

An ancient fishing technique known as the 'Almadraba' has been practised for over 3000 years in an area close to the Strait of Gibraltar, off the coast of the Spanish province of Andalusia. Tuna unfortunate enough to encounter these fishermen are forced to follow a net which runs from the sea into the coast and a maze of other nets which lead into a series of enclosures, eventually ending up in a central chamber called the 'copo'. The frantic tuna are herded into the copo and the floor of the net is raised, trapping the animals. They are then slaughtered as they are brought closer to the surface. Boats surround the net and the fish are hauled onto the vessels by the fishermen, who attack the animals with hooks and spears. The waters quickly turn red with blood.

This ancient method of catching bluefin tuna is still practised today, although the industry has largely moved on and the general scale of bluefin tuna fishing has increased dramatically over recent decades. The techniques used to catch the now highly sought-after bluefin tuna have modernised to ensure that the fishing operation is now so efficient that the animals do not stand a chance.

As if it was not enough that large-scale industrial fishing is supported by the latest modern technology, an increasing amount of fishermen are resorting to illegal activities to secure their catches. Illegal fishing in the Mediterranean Sea has reached such astronomical proportions that it is now estimated that around half of the bluefin tuna caught in the region are caught illegally. Despite numerous regulations, international treaties, and even specific protected areas, a total lack of adequate enforcement ensures the continuation of this outrageous situation. Every day, thousands of vessels set out onto the Mediterranean Sea, deploying huge purse seine fishing nets, driftnets or longlines. The sea is so heavily exploited that it is not just the bluefin tuna which is under threat: it is only a matter of time before the fragile populations of other species become endangered. Parliaments around Europe have been united in their unwillingness to effectively tackle these problems, resulting in half-measures which do nothing to alleviate this dire situation.

MEET THE PURSE SEINERS

There are various methods used in the fishing of bluefin tuna. Purse seine is a method used to catch tuna and other pelagic (open sea) species, such as sardines. In the case of tuna fishing, an entire school of fish is first trapped in a net, then both ends of the net are pulled together to create a cylinder shape. A line fed through rings along the bottom of the net is then pulled tight, closing the net like a purse, and preventing the fish from sounding (swimming down) to escape capture. In many cases, the tuna fish are then transferred from the seine net into a transfer cage, which is then pulled by a tug to a local or distant tuna farm for fattening.

In the period of 1996 to 2006, purse seiners were responsible for 50% of all bluefin catches in the Mediterranean. In the last five years, this number has increased to nearly 70%. Looking at the total number of purse seine vessels which currently

"THE GENERAL SCALE OF BLUEFIN TUNA FISHING HAS INCREASED DRAMATICALLY OVER RECENT DECADES."

> "PARLIAMENTS AROUND EUROPE HAVE BEEN UNITED IN THEIR UNWILLINGNESS TO EFFECTIVELY TACKLE THESE PROBLEMS."

operate in the region, their catch capacity is over double the annual quotas set by the ICCAT, the international commission tasked with managing the tuna fishing industry. Over 250 new purse seine vessels have been constructed since 2007 and these now make up nearly 40% of the entire fleet.

A report by the WWF estimated that in 2008, 614 purse seine vessels were operating in the Mediterranean Sea with the intention of catching bluefin. Forty percent of these vessels were Turkish-flagged, while other major fleets included Italian, Croatian and Libyan vessels. The huge investment in the expansion of the purse seine fleet over the past ten years has to be recouped somehow and unfortunately this is being achieved through reckless (and often illegal) overfishing. The transfer of bluefin to other vessels at sea goes largely unnoticed and all countries catch well in excess of their permitted quotas. The industrial scale and efficiency

"LOOKING AT THE TOTAL NUMBER OF PURSE SEINE VESSELS WHICH CURRENTLY OPERATE IN THE REGION, THEIR CATCH CAPACITY IS OVER DOUBLE THE ANNUAL QUOTAS."

of the purse seine fleets is directly responsible for the overfishing of the bluefin populations.

The biggest fleet catching bluefin tuna in the Mediterranean is from Turkey. Many of the vessels operating out of Turkey are known to be engaged in illegal fishing practices and independent sources have verified that most catches go unreported.

ICCAT regulations state a minimum legal landing size of 30 kg (66 lbs), which allows the bluefin tuna to enjoy at least one reproduction cycle before being killed. However, Turkish and Italian media have in recent years reported the landing of many juvenile bluefin, prior to their first spawning. This continued landing of fish under the minimum size limit is bringing the end of the tuna fishing in the Mediterranean Sea closer than ever.

The misreporting of catches is a long-standing issue in the Mediterranean. One of the reasons that ICCAT has been a hugely ineffective instrument to manage the fishing industry is that for years, countries have been supplying incorrect or insufficient data regarding bluefin catches and this falsification has gone unchallenged.

"TRANSFER OF BLUEFIN TO OTHER VESSELS AT SEA GOES LARGELY UNNOTICED AND ALL COUNTRIES CATCH WELL IN EXCESS OF THEIR PERMITTED QUOTAS"

In some cases, catch information has not been supplied at all. In the case of Turkey, the use of fraudulent catch data is widespread.

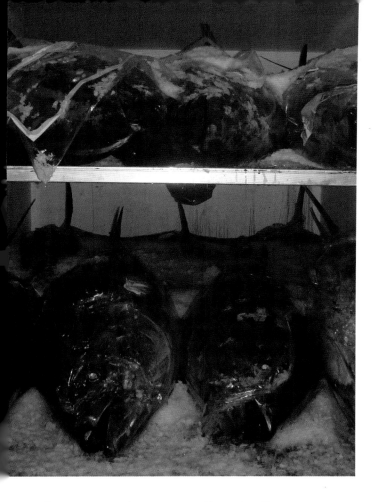

For example, according to the numbers given to ICCAT by the Turkish government in 2008, the total bluefin tuna catch made by the Turkish fleet that year was 879 metric tonnes. This is 99% of the total catch quota of 887 metric tonnes allocated to Turkey for that year. Aside from the numerous illegal vessels operating as part of the fleet, the Turkish government acknowledges having issued fishing licenses for at least 98 fishing vessels, the majority of which are purse seiners of 30 to 50 metres in length and with a capacity of 200 to 300 metric tonnes. You only have to multiply the number of vessels by their tonnage to see that the numbers just do not add up. Turkey's ongoing harbouring of illegal vessels, unreported catches and landing of juveniles will lead to the extinction of the bluefin tuna in the near future unless drastic action is taken, and fast.

Italy is another shocking story. This country accounts for about 17% of the total purse seine fleet in the Mediterranean and is the second worst contributor to the great Mediterranean purse seine pandemic. Since 1997, Italy has built 27 new vessels, bringing its total active fleet up to 60 purse seiners during these last few years. The total capacity of the Italian purse seine fleet is just over 7,500 metric tonnes, about 14% of the entire potential bluefin catch in the Mediterranean. This tonnage is also double Italy's 2007 ICCAT quota.

The largest catch of the Italian fleet was declared in 1997, which has raised suspicions about the under-reporting of catches since then, as the fleet has definitely grown in size, capacity and efficiency over the past 14 years. An independent study of four Italian purse seiners found that each had caught over three times their individual vessel quotas for 2001. Out of all EU countries, Italy is the worst offender when it comes to under-reporting catches and overfishing, landing up to an estimated three times its quota every year. Other countries which operate substantial purse seine fleets include France, Croatia and Tunisia, the latter of which was exposed by the WWF as operating largely illegally.

> "AN INDEPENDENT STUDY OF FOUR ITALIAN PURSE SEINERS FOUND THAT EACH HAD CAUGHT OVER THREE TIMES THEIR INDIVIDUAL VESSEL QUOTAS FOR 2001."

DRIFTNETS

Another fishing technique which is used to catch tuna is driftnets. The use of these nets is still common practice around the world, including in the Mediterranean. Driftnets pose a major threat to marine wildlife. These 'curtains of death' can be kilometres in length, catching everything that lies in their path, including much unwanted bycatch – fish, birds, turtles, whales, dolphins and other species that are caught, often killed and wasted unintentionally while attempting to catch a specific fish. Driftnets are particularly dangerous for cetaceans, such as whales and dolphins, which need to surface in order to breathe.

> "THE UNITED NATIONS BANNED THE USE OF DRIFTNETS ON THE HIGH SEAS IN 1992, BUT THEIR USE IS STILL WIDESPREAD."

In recognition of the destructiveness of this fishing method, the United Nations banned the use of driftnets on the high seas in 1992, but their use remains widespread. In many parts of the Mediterranean, where the habitats of fin whales, sperm whales, sharks, turtles and numerous dolphin species are located, the presence of driftnets more often than not has fatal consequences. In one report analysing the total catch of Spanish driftnetters in 1994, it was found that only 7% of the catch was the targeted species. The remaining 93% was made up of thousands of now dead turtles, sharks and dolphins.

While the global UN driftnet ban of 1992 already covered most of the Mediterranean, it was not enforced. In 1997, the EU passed a separate ban, prohibiting the use of driftnets longer than 2.5 kilometres or to catch certain species, such as bluefin tuna, swordfish and albacore. However, it would take another five years for the ban to actually come into force for all EU-registered vessels - on 1 January 2002. As recently as 2007, amendments were made to the Agreement on the Conservation of Cetaceans of the Black Sea and

93% unwanted bycatch

7% Target species

Mediterranean Sea (ACCOBAMS) to once again ban the use of driftnets. Since 1989, numerous rules and regulations have been passed by the UN, IWC, EU, GFCM, ICCAT, CFCM and within ACCOBAMS to ban the use of these nets. Italy, Turkey, Algeria, Tunisia and Morocco have fleets which continue to use the illegal nets, even after repeated calls to stop the practice and with infringement procedures from the European Commission in progress. With an absence of anyone to physically enforce the ban, these driftnets continue to be used. Thousands of sharks and turtles and an estimated 10,000 cetaceans are killed by driftnets in the Mediterranean every year.

FRANCE

France has been one of the main culprits when it comes to illegal driftnet use. The fishing method is called 'thonaille' in French and its use dates back to ancient times - when the technique was called 'courantille' and the bluefin could still be found very close to the coast. This method of coastal fishing became obsolete when the tuna populations around the French coastline disappeared in the 1960s and the fishery was expanded to go further out to sea. When the UN driftnet ban came into force in 1992, the EEC (now the EU) approved a similar ban, prohibiting the use of nets longer than 2.5 kilometres (1.5 miles) in European waters. This primarily affected the Italian fleet as the French fleet was already fishing with shorter nets. The French were, however, affected by a second EU ban, which came into force in 2002. Besides length restrictions, it also banned the use of the nets to catch certain species such as bluefin tuna, swordfish and albacore. Instead of receiving EU subsidies to switch to a different type of fishing gear and then continuing regardless with the illegal use of driftnets, like the Italians had done, the French fishermen found another way to circumvent the ban. Backed by their government, they exploited a loophole in the EU legislation which did not clearly define what a driftnet actually is. The French government appealed the decision taken by the EU while they continued to use the driftnets illegally. They also passed a decree that authorised the operation of their thonaille vessels under 'special fishing permits'. The decision violated EU rules and when three conservation organisations took the government to court over the issue, the government decision was overruled. Nevertheless, this did not stop the French government from continuing to issue fishing quotas to the illegal driftnetters. Thousands of cetaceans, sharks and turtles died in French driftnets in the time the French government spent arguing that the thonailles and driftnets were different types of nets. This also went on inside the protected Pelagos Sanctuary, north of Sardinia, which is inhabited by the endangered fin whales, sperm whales and pilot whales, as well as various dolphin species.

> **THOUSANDS OF CETACEANS, SHARKS AND TURTLES DIED IN FRENCH DRIFTNETS IN THE TIME THE FRENCH GOVERNMENT SPENT ARGUING THAT THE THONAILLES AND DRIFTNETS WERE DIFFERENT TYPES OF NETS.**

It would take until 2007 for the EU Fisheries Council to pass new legislation, leaving no doubt as to what constitutes a driftnet, effectively banning the use of all thonaillers. Three weeks before the new regulations came into force, the French Ministry for Agriculture and Fisheries allocated generous quotas to the driftnet fleet. In 2007, conservation organisation Oceana concluded from observations that the French fleet consisted of 92 thonaille vessels and that a quarter of the fleet had entered into service after the EU driftnet ban came into force in 2002. Some of these vessels were even constructed using funds from the FIFG, the now reformed EU fisheries funding programme, after the EU driftnet ban had come into effect. On top of the continued increase in the number of vessels, Oceana observed driftnets on the docks at some ports which were not supposed to host driftnet vessels. This indicates that driftnets may be kept aboard vessels that are registered to use a different fishing method, but the operators may choose to use the illegal nets opportunistically when out at sea. The French have greatly scaled down their use of illegal driftnets, but it is thought that a small number of fishermen continue to use the nets to this day.

ITALY

Over the last 15 years, Italy has received millions of Euros in grants from the EU to eliminate the illegal use of driftnets by its swordfish fleet. Somewhat disappointingly and yet unsurprisingly, the illegal use of these nets continues, regardless of the subsidies. Vessels use fishing gear other than that permitted under their fishing permits and many vessels are now converted so that they can opportunistically switch to different types of fishing gear - including driftnets - while at sea. The first EU regulation limiting the use of driftnets, coming into force in 1992, had a significant economic impact on the Italian swordfish driftnet fleet. It was decided that funds were to be allocated to Italy through the FIFG to dismantle and convert its driftnet fleet, which numbered around 700 vessels during its heydey in the 1990s. The conversion was largely voluntary, which meant that most vessels continued to use the nets. Various new regulations were passed, but it was not until a second EU driftnet ban was on the cards that the Italian government was given a new stimulus to dismantle and convert its driftnet fleet. During the period from 1997 to 1999, €98 million (US

$132 million) were allocated for this purpose. In 2000, it seemed that around 85% of the driftnet vessels had been converted to other fishing gear. After 2002, once the new ban was already in force, the Italian government announced that a further €5 million (US $6.7 million) was to be paid out for the conversion of the remaining 100 vessels which continued to operate illegally. The money was given to the driftnetters with few checks and, unsurprisingly, nothing much happened. It is estimated that 137 Italian driftnetters continue to operate illegally to this day. Italy's non-compliance with the driftnet ban has resulted in an infringement procedure, initiated by the European Commission. The United States has warned Italy that its fishing products will be banned from import

if the illegal driftnet operations continue. It is also believed that many driftnets and other equipment were sold to Morocco after the measures to stop driftnet use by Italian vessels were implemented in the period from 1995 to 2000. Consequently, as measures were introduced in Italy, a sharp increase in the use of driftnets was observed in Morocco. Equipped with these driftnets, the country quickly became the second largest provider of swordfish in the Mediterranean, while roughly 65% of swordfish from the Moroccan fishery now ends up on Italian markets.

> Stopping the illegal use of driftnets in the Mediterranean Sea is a top priority for The Black Fish. The Mediterranean Sea is one of the most unique yet fragile marine eco-systems in the world. A place where illegal driftnets simply don't belong.
>
> **JOIN US** in our upcoming driftnet campaign. See **www.theblackfish.org/driftnets** for more information.

ALONG THE LINES OF DEATH AND DESTRUCTION

Another highly destructive fishing technique is the longline. A longline is a line with thousands of baited hooks, targeting mostly swordfish, bluefin tuna, albacore and hake. As the baited hooks are indiscriminate, longlines represent a major threat to marine wildlife. Sea birds, such as shearwaters and albatrosses, get caught up in the lines and drown. Yearly, thousands of dead turtles, dolphins and sharks are pulled up, strangled by the lines. Various international regulations and resolutions have been passed in an attempt to limit the damage done by these lines, but so far to little effect. In the Mediterranean, an important habitat for migratory species such as swordfish and tuna, the use of longlines poses a serious threat. Longlines are used by fleets from all around the Mediterranean. As some fishermen in the region opportunistically change their type of fishing gear, the number of longline vessels is in constant flux. Longlining is an incredibly wasteful operation, killing thousands of animals, some of which are critically endangered and protected. These include the loggerhead turtle, the Mediterranean populations of which are struggling to survive. Every year, more than 250,000 endangered loggerhead and leatherback turtles are caught in longlines worldwide. Around half of turtles who come in contact with the lines do not survive. The shark is another common victim of the longline swordfish fishery. The blue and mako sharks, both classed as 'near endangered', are regularly found on the lines. As one WWF report states: "from 1990-2000, Portuguese swordfish longliners in the North Atlantic caught around 3 metric tonnes of blue shark for every 1 metric tonne of swordfish. Similarly, blue shark and mako shark made up 68% of landings by Spanish swordfish longliners in the Atlantic Ocean in 1999, while blue shark made up around 25% of landings by Spanish swordfish longliners in the Mediterranean." An estimated 100,000 sharks are currently killed every year by the large Moroccan driftnet and longline fleets, catching an average of one shark for every two swordfish.

Longline fishing is also a major threat to sea birds, regularly catching gannets, fulmars, gulls and various species of shearwater. In 1997, it was

reported that 200 Cory's shearwaters were killed by a single Spanish longline vessel in one day. The Spanish, Italian and Greek longline fleets find thousands of dead sea birds in their lines every year. White and blue marlin are further bycatch species that are also often found on longlines. Over 95% of the total catches of marlins are taken as

> "FROM 1990-2000, PORTUGUESE SWORDFISH LONGLINERS IN THE NORTH ATLANTIC CAUGHT AROUND 3 METRIC TONNES OF BLUE SHARK FOR EVERY 1 METRIC TONNE OF SWORDFISH."

bycatch in longline fisheries targeting swordfish and tuna. As a result of this collateral overfishing, both of thesemarlin species are increasingly under threat. Their Atlantic population is believed to have reduced by 80% over the past 50 years. The white marlin population is currently only 6% of its pre-longlining (1960s) abundance and declining by 3% every year.

CATCHING THE THIEF

It is clear that many of the fishing techniques used are overtly destructive and in many cases cause great damage to wildlife and ecosystems beyond the effects on the populations that are killed for consumption. There are no Economic Exclusion Zones (EEZ) in the Mediterranean and the jurisdictional waters extend less than twelve miles from the coast in places, such as around Turkey and Cyprus. The majority of the fishing grounds are therefore located in international waters and shared by many countries, with the responsibility to properly

manage the fishery left to bodies with no real enforcement powers, such as the International Commission for the Conservation of Atlantic Tunas (ICCAT).

The French Navy is one of the few navies tasked with patrolling international waters during the busy summer fishing seasons. The navy patrol boat "Arago" occasionally inspects tuna fishing vessels during this period. In one operation, where 24 boats in the Eastern Mediterranean were subjected to surprise visits, the Turkish were found to be the biggest culprits when it came to bending the rules. The Navy report stated: "The

> "IN 1997, IT WAS REPORTED THAT 200 CORY'S SHEARWATERS WERE KILLED BY A SINGLE SPANISH LONGLINE VESSEL IN ONE DAY."

Turkish didn't seem to apply the regulations. Registration documents were either not filled in or simply did not exist. There are no ICCAT observers in the purse seiners or the vessels are simply not registered with ICCAT." ICCAT rules state that every vessel larger than 24 metres must carry a regional observer. The French found only one observer across the entire fleet, and they raised question marks about his honesty: "After the inspections he would find all sorts of explanations or false arguments to try to justify non-compliance with ICCAT recommendations. Moreover, the estimations of the amount of fish in the cages given by him were on average 10 times lower than those estimated by the navy divers." During the operation, the French Navy detailed some 22 breaches of ICCAT regulations. These included unlicensed fishing, poor or absent record-keeping and the landing of juvenile bluefin.

The findings of this French Navy patrol are good examples of the problems facing the lucrative bluefin tuna industry. There is some enforcement, though it is very little compared to the total amount of fishing activity that occurs. The lack of adequate enforcement, together with the high profits which can be made from bluefin tuna, means poachers are willing to take the risk to continue their illegal operations. The bizarre thing is that all the regulations are in place to monitor and control the fishing activities in the Mediterranean Sea. If governments took charge of their responsibility and upheld the laws which they themselves have undersigned, the bluefin tuna population would never have reached this critical point.

> "IF GOVERNMENTS UPHELD THE LAWS WHICH THEY THEMSELVES HAVE UNDERSIGNED, THE BLUEFIN TUNA WOULD NEVER HAVE REACHED THIS CRITICAL POINT."

FARMING FISHES

Yes, fish can be farmed, too. The farming of bluefin tuna, however, is not really farming as it is generally understood; it is more like ranching. Regular farming includes the reproduction of the animal stock with little need for new animals to come into the farm from the wild or elsewhere. When involving aquatic animals this is called aquaculture (or sometimes mariculture when in seawater). In the case of the bluefin tuna, every single animal in the sea pens and cages has been caught from the wild, meaning that traditional tuna farming does not involve any reproduction of the fish. Bluefin tuna farming subtracts from the wild population of bluefin and so does nothing to protect it, but rather contributes to its depletion. Many juvenile bluefins are caught and brought to the farms for fattening and slaughter before ever getting a chance to reproduce. This has had catastrophic effects on the bluefin tuna population.

WHY AND HOW

The first bluefin tuna farm appeared in the year 1996, off the coast of Spain in the Mediterranean. Other tuna species had previously been farmed (or ranched) elsewhere, such as the Southern bluefin tuna, Thunnus Maccoyii, off the coast of Australia. In just a few years, the farming of bluefin tuna in the Mediterranean region had become a large-scale industry. Nowadays, nearly all bluefin tuna caught by purse seine boats in the Mediterranean are brought to tuna farms. In 2005, just nine years after the first farm was built, close to 90% of the total allowable catch (an estimated 28,450 metric tonnes) of bluefin in the Mediterranean was taken to farming facilities after capture. To go from killing the full number of bluefin in the catch quota upon capture to farming 90% of all bluefins caught in less than a decade is a remarkable development. This was partly sponsored by European Union subsidies for aquaculture, even though it is, strictly speaking, not aquaculture, as no reproduction occurs. According to an estimation by the WWF, some €20 million (US $27 million) of European taxpayers' money was spent on developing bluefin farms, and therefore the decimation of the wild bluefin populations, between 1997 and 2004.

The main reason bluefins are kept alive and fed is to increase the fat content of their muscles, since the more fat they contain, the more the traders, and therefore end-consumers, are willing to pay. The bluefins are caught during the spawning season, at which time the fish will have expended considerable amounts of energy and thus reduced the natural levels of fat in their bodies. Lean fish simply will not sell. Another reason why farming is popular is that it helps to avoid flooding the market during the short summer fishing season, thus ensuring a better price by supplying bluefin all year round. For Croatian farmers, who are allowed to catch bluefins weighing as little as eight kilograms (17.5 lbs), the farming is intended to bring the fish up to a market size of 30-50 kilograms (66 to 110 lbs).

"SOME €20 MILLION (US $27 MILLION) OF EUROPEAN TAXPAYERS' MONEY WAS SPENT ON DEVELOPING BLUEFIN FARMS BETWEEN 1997 AND 2004."

When a school of bluefin is found travelling, feeding or spawning near the surface, a purse seiner will move in and encircle the school with its net, trapping the fish in its huge net purse. The purse is then attached to a much smaller transport cage, into which the fish are transferred. The transport cage, some 50 metres in diameter and 20 metres deep, is then towed to a farming facility by a tug boat travelling at a steady 1 to 1.5 knots, while the purse seiner is free to move on to catch another school. This transport to the farm costs around €2,000 to €3,000 (US $2,700 to $4,000) per day and can take several weeks, during which the fish are fed to reduce mortality and begin the fattening process. However, being tugged through the sea is traumatic for the bluefins and after being transferred once again into a second pen at their final destination, they need a period of 10 to 14 days to calm down before the full fattening operation can start.

The bluefins are then kept at the farms for about three to seven months, but smaller ones can be kept for up to two years. As a result of their high metabolism, body temperature and constant need to swim to oxygenate through their gills, these fish require a lot of energy in their diet. They must be fed large amounts of feed in order to grow and store fat. The feed conversion ratios (FCR) for the bluefin tuna are difficult to pinpoint precisely, since the initial size and weight of the fish upon capture can only be estimated. Bluefins are easily stressed and therefore cannot be weighed and measured upon arrival to a farm, since the risk of them dying from the stress caused by handling is high. The feed conversion ratios have, however, been narrowed down to between 10:1 to 15:1 for smaller bluefins and 15:1 to 20:1 for bigger ones. This means that the bluefin will gain 1 kg (2.2 lbs) of body weight for every 10 to 20kg (22

to 44 lbs) of smaller fish the bluefin consume. The development of tuna farming has caused an increase in quotas for the smaller fish, required to nourish the farmed tuna. This is putting strain on the populations of these smaller species, including sardine, herring, mackerel and squid, most of which are already overfished in their own right. The farms in the Mediterranean mostly feed bluefins using imported feed, although some use smaller, locally-caught fish, such as anchovies.

ENVIRONMENTAL IMPACTS

The bluefin tuna are held in circular or rectangular floating offshore net cages. The high concentration of uneaten, wasted "feed fish" (dead smaller fish fed to the bluefin while in captivity) and fish faeces causes pollution and poses a potential danger to the local environment and ecosystems. The constant input of nutrients in the surrounding area as a result of the feed used to nourish the bluefin causes a disturbance and changes the living conditions for the organisms in that area. Most of the bluefin farms are still relatively small, but larger farms of established aquaculture species, such as salmon, are known to create dead zones on the seabed surrounding them, where currents are unable to flush away the waste. Even if currents dilute the waste from the farms, they are still adding to the general pollution of the sea. To provide one example: in 2002, the same amount of nitrogen waste as that contained in the untreated sewage water of 3.2 million people was produced and released into the marine environment by the Scottish salmon farming industry alone.

"THE DEVELOPMENT OF TUNA FARMING HAS CAUSED AN INCREASE IN QUOTAS FOR SMALLER FISH, WHICH ARE NEEDED TO FEED THE TUNA IN THE FARMS."

Research is continuing on how to make the bluefin tuna a true aquaculture species, meaning the whole lifecycle of the fish would be controlled since it would be bred and raised in captivity. If this were to be achieved on an industrial scale, new threats to the environment and the wild bluefin tuna would follow, similar to those that are already the case in other established aquaculture facilities. When fish, like other animals, are kept in crowded conditions, there is a heightened risk of outbreaks of disease and parasitic infection.

outbreak. If a moderate outbreak in the wild population should reach a farm, it is likely this will become an epidemic due to the unnatural conditions in a farming facility. Environmental effects of salmon farming, including the spread of deadly diseases, parasitic outbreaks and genetic degradation, have already heavily afflicted the wild salmon populations. The risk of wild salmon being attacked by sea lice (a parasite that eats salmon flesh) has been studied near an infected farm in British Colombia, Canada. The risk

> "ENVIRONMENTAL EFFECTS OF SALMON FARMING, INCLUDING THE SPREAD OF DEADLY DISEASES, PARASITIC OUTBREAKS AND GENETIC DEGRADATION, HAVE HEAVILY AFFLICTED THE WILD SALMON POPULATIONS."

Antibiotics and parasiticides are used to improve the health of fish in farms, but these spread into the environment and threaten the immune systems of other marine life not associated with the farms.

There are several ways for pathogens and parasites to be transmitted between farmed and wild populations. Fish escaping from farms can carry infections to the wild populations and wild fish passing by a farm may also fall victim to high levels of disease there was found to be up to 73 times greater than normal and on the particular farm in the study these levels remained heightened within three kilometres (two miles) of the farm along two migration routes for wild salmon. Given the fact that the risk of infection increased so greatly in the single, defined area in which the research farm was located, imagine what this could mean for the wild bluefin if the number of farms in the Mediterranean were to increase.

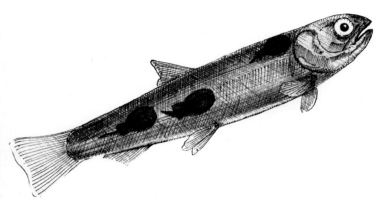

The results of other research on the environmental impact of salmon aquaculture were printed in the scientific journal *Nature* in 2002: "The offspring of farmed fish, some data suggests, are often unable to complete the heroic salmon runs by which the natural species navigate between spawning grounds inland and breeding grounds in the ocean. Critics say that, together with the rampant transmission of lice and disease from fish farms to natural stocks, the result is that the very survival of natural salmon runs in countries such as Scotland, Canada and Norway is now threatened".

The increase in tuna farming in the Mediterranean poses a similar threat to the migrating bluefin tuna. If the industry's long-desired aquaculture of the species is achieved, then the threat posed will increase even further: escapees mating with wild bluefins could greatly damage the diversity of the gene pool, as is already happening to the wild populations of Atlantic salmon.

The impact of farming carnivorous fish stretches beyond the one species that is farmed. It puts pressure on other fisheries to produce the fish fed to the farmed stocks. The shipping of feed fish to farm areas can also cause diseases to be transmitted between populations, as happened in the 1990s when feed fish shipped to tuna farms in Australia caused an outbreak that decimated local populations of sardine and pilchard.

WILL AQUACULTURE BE ABLE TO SAVE THE BLUEFIN?

Aquaculture is a significant, fast-growing sector of the world food economy. Around half of all seafood on the global market today was produced on a farm. Some argue that aquaculture will be the salvation of species threatened with extinction due to the overfishing of wild populations, including the bluefin tuna. No-one can predict the future,

> "IT WOULD BE A GRAVE MISTAKE TO CONTINUE TO SEE AQUACULTURE AS THE SOLUTION TO TODAY'S PROBLEMS, WITHOUT LOOKING AT THE UNDERLYING ISSUE OF THE INCREASING MARKET DEMAND FOR SEAFOOD."

but we can acknowledge past mistakes and learn important lessons that allow us to avoid making the same mistakes all over again.

What is claimed to be the salvation of the wild bluefin has already been hailed as the salvation of wild salmon. Among the carnivorous finfish species in aquaculture, the Atlantic salmon is the one produced in the greatest numbers and serves as a good indicator of what problems can be expected when culturing other carnivorous species. Aquaculturing is supposed to release the pressure on wild stocks, increasing the amount of farmed fish on the market and thus decreasing the need to catch wild fish. Looking back at the recent history of salmon production, we find that even though the amount of farmed salmon has drastically increased and now greatly exceeds the amount of wild salmon on the market, the catches of wild salmon are higher now than they were when farmed salmon accounted for only one percent of total global salmon output. The rapidly growing aquaculture has not decreased the pressure on the wild populations at all. The populations of wild salmon are in worse shape today than they were before the 1970s, when aquaculture first started to supply salmon to an international market.

Without a drastic change in the way aquaculture works, it will never save the bluefin tuna. At the same time, we are putting increasing pressure on the other species that are already heavily overfished to feed these captive stocks. It would be a grave mistake to continue to see aquaculture as the solution to today's problems, without looking at the underlying issue of the increasing market demand for seafood. What the oceans can offer us is finite and it is important that we treat any 'solution' that proposes to continue to meet this ever-growing market demand with extreme caution.

CHAPTER FIVE

FISHY BUSINESS

Around the world there has been a huge increase in the numbers and capacity of industrial fishing fleets since the 1960s, largely due to technological advancements in industrial fishing gear. Fish prices have dropped, demand has risen and, as a result, the bluefin tuna populations off the coast of Brazil and in the North Sea have been heavily depleted. Since these fishing areas have been all but exhausted, attention has moved onto other waters and now the tuna populations in the eastern Mediterranean and western Atlantic are also under strain. In 1966, seventeen countries signed the International Convention for the Conservation of Atlantic Tunas. The aim of the Convention was "to co-operate in maintaining the populations of tuna and tuna-like fishes at levels which will permit the maximum sustainable catch for food and other purposes." The Convention also planned to set up a commission which could make recommendations on catch quotas on the basis of all scientific evidence available, unless a majority of the signatory states should raise an objection. In the last 40 years, this latter option seems to have become common practice, with disastrous consequences for the bluefin tuna.

INTERNATIONAL CONSPIRACY TO CATCH ALL TUNA (ICCAT)

The bluefin business is a lucrative one and has only been able to continue its destructive work at the grace of various political institutions that allow the ongoing harvesting of this endangered fish to continue. The International Commission for the Conservation of Atlantic Tunas (ICCAT) is where most decisions regarding the bluefin fishery are made. Since 1969, the Commission has been trusted to regulate and protect, among other species, the Atlantic bluefin tuna.

The ICCAT is made up of a Commission, Council, Executive Secretary, and different subject area panels, all of which are responsible for the co-ordination and implementation of scientific investigations and subsequent regulatory recommendations, which are submitted for approval by representatives of the member states at the ICCAT annual general meetings. The ICCAT also employs a small group of scientific staff. This group, known as the Standing Committee on Research and Statistics (SCRC), is responsible for analysing scientific data on the health of fish stocks to make recommendations on the annual catch quotas.

EXPRESS TRAIN TO EXTINCTION

The problem is that ICCAT is a political organisation and its member states, which are generally the same that are exploiting the wild populations of bluefin, are making political decisions, not scientific ones. The Commission has consistently set catch quotas well above the advice of their own scientists. These have, among other things, directly contributed the demise of bluefin tuna populations. The Commission has been unable to properly regulate the

> "ICCAT HAS CONSISTENTLY SET CATCH QUOTAS WELL ABOVE THE ADVICE OF THEIR OWN SCIENTISTS."

industry, thus it is not without reason that the Commission is often satirically dubbed the 'International Conspiracy to Catch All Tuna'. However, it cannot be held solely responsible for the current crisis, given the great number of other active players.

Before the 1970s, the bluefin tuna market was considerably modest, mainly because outside of Japan, bluefin tuna meat was primarily

used for dog and cat food and not considered the same delicacy for human consumption that it is today. Following World War II, Japan adopted the development of refrigeration. The new practice of preserving fish for a longer period of time has changed eating habits and led to an increase in the consumption of raw fish.

Bluefin tuna in particular, served as sushi and sashimi, has consequently experienced a sharp rise in popularity. Japan's demand for bluefin exploded in the 1980s, a result of which was the dramatic depletion of bluefin in its own waters. Eyes turned to an important spawning area for the fish, the Mediterranean Sea, where populations were still plentiful. In the 1990s bluefin tuna became valuable outside of Japan and its popularity grew in the form of sushi the world over.

"BEFORE THE 1970S, BLUEFIN TUNA MEAT WAS NOT CONSIDERED THE SAME DELICACY AS IT IS TODAY AND WAS PRIMARILY USED FOR DOG AND CAT FOOD"

In order to meet the demands of this booming market, the European Union began granting subsidies to the European tuna fishing industry. This led to a renovation and expansion of the European tuna fleet. By 1998 the average purse seiner was twice as long and four times as powerful as equivalent ships back in the 1970s, and by 2008, more than one fifth of all vessels registered with ICCAT to catch bluefin tuna were paid for by the EU.

"Amongst the top receivers of EU fisheries subsidies are the EU fleet of tuna purse-seiners fishing outside EU waters, including through FPAs." (Fishsubsidy.org)

Given the fact that Japan is estimated to consume nearly 80% of the world catches of bluefin tuna, the European tuna fishery is mainly geared towards the export market. By the mid-1990s, concerns had begun to arise regarding the status of the bluefin stock in the Mediterranean, and ICCAT had begun to set country-specific fishing quotas, including TACs and other measures to limit the fishing for bluefin tuna. TAC stands for Total Allowable Catch and is one of a number of quota systems used by institutions such as the ICCAT. TACs are controversial as they are based upon the total 'available' fish, as well as the traditional share of the catch that has been allotted to a specific country. Many scientists have criticised their use as dated and an ineffective system to conserve and manage the fisheries in light of the current crisis.

Compliance with the new rules set by ICCAT in the 1990s was so poor that in the following decade the subsidised European fleet caught twice the amounts permitted under the ICCAT quotas. For example, the bluefin quota approved by ICCAT representatives in 2003 and 2006 was 32,000 metric tonnes a year. The estimates of the actual catches put these closer to 50,000 metric tonnes. In those same years, ICCAT's own scientists at the SCRS strongly advised against exceeding the annual quotas by 15,000 metric tonnes for the bluefin simply to be permitted any chance of survival, let alone regenerate its population to a sustainable size. While ignoring warnings about over-quota catches from their own scientists, these governments were aware that certain fishing operations bypassed the mandatory declaration of catches, as well as taking in ever-increasing numbers of tuna, including smaller schools of fish.

> "INCREASINGLY TUNA WOULD BE TRANSFERRED ONTO REFRIGERATED VESSELS AT SEA, WITHOUT EVER ENTERING A EUROPEAN PORT FOR INSPECTION.

Spotting planes were deployed for more effective detection of tuna schools, while increasingly tuna would be transferred onto refrigerated Japanese vessels at sea. The fish would be slaughtered on-board, without the vessel ever entering a European port for inspection or declaration of the catch. Meanwhile, even when certain EU member states, such as France, were accused of failing to meet their obligations to establish certain control measures for fishing activities in 1991, inspections, measurements and other enforcement continued to be so sporadic that France was accused of the same charges a second time in 2005.

"The judgement from the European Court of Justice (ECJ) in case C-304/-02, Commission v. France, has provided the Community with a clear confirmation of the role and obligations of Member States with regard to control and enforcement of CFP rules. Following this ruling, France was ordered to pay a lump sum of 20 million Euro and a periodic six-month penalty of EUR 57,761,250."
(Official Journal of the European Union/SPECIAL REPORT No 7/2007)

In 2006, the scientists and policy makers at ICCAT therefore came to conclusion that bluefin tuna was at a 'high risk of fishery and stock collapse'. Misguidance and the lack of effective management and organised execution of ICCAT activities and quotas were listed as the main reasons.

unabated without effective enforcement. The illegal fishing activity reached an astronomical scale, peaking at an estimated 60,000 metric tonnes in 2007. All in all, between 1998 and 2007 an estimated one third of all bluefin tuna caught in the Mediterranean Sea was taken illegally, either caught over

> "BETWEEN 1998 AND 2007 AN ESTIMATED ONE THIRD OF ALL BLUEFIN TUNA CAUGHT IN THE MEDITERRANEAN SEA WAS TAKEN ILLEGALLY."

ICCAT AND THE QUOTA CIRCUS

Following their admittance of the problems, ICCAT released a 15-year management plan for the recovery of bluefin stocks. Championed by the EU, the plan included a catch level of 29,500 metric tonnes for 2006 with gradual annual reductions in quota to 25,500 metric tonnes by 2010. It also proposed closing the fishing season before the peak spawning period in June and increasing the minimum size to 30kg (66 lbs), with certain exceptions for farming operations.

Good intentions aside, the catching of undersized fish as well as the misreporting of catches continued

the allowed quota or by catching undersized fish. This created a black market for the increasingly valuable fish, estimated to be worth around €700 million (approx. US $1 billion).

In 2008, the quota was lowered to 22,000 metric tonnes for 2009 and 13,500 metric tonnes for 2010. The ICCAT also introduced new enforcement measures and bans in order to more effectively prevent illegal overfishing, as well as the fishing of undersized bluefin tuna. These measures included a ban on transshipments at sea, the posting of observers on fishing boats and at fish farms, as well as the introduction of a document-based tracking system to track the fish up the supply chain.

"There was just no political will to enforce the rules, most notably the quota. Until 2008 there was no enforcement. No one declared [their catch]. There was general cheating."
(Jean-Marc Fromentin, marine biologist and a member of ICCAT's SCRS)

The new improvements in monitoring and control were praised by the European Commission for helping to ensure complete and reliable traceability of the fish. According to reports from independent investigators, it turned out to be another system filled with loopholes. In many cases important documents and catch reports intended to ensure the legality of the catch were suddenly 'missing', or erroneous. In other instances, catch documents pertaining to different catches from different locations appeared to consist of fish with the exact same weight and size.

The irresponsibility of ICCAT in setting unsustainable quotas and permitting unscrupulous fishing practices to continue over a number of years, as well as the lack of cooperation and willingness to provide legal enforcement from its members, have

"IN MANY CASES, IMPORTANT DOCUMENTS AND CATCH REPORTS INTENDED TO ENSURE THE LEGALITY OF THE CATCH WERE SUDDENLY 'MISSING' OR ERRONEOUS."

pushed the bluefin tuna closer to extinction. At this moment even an annual quota of 8,000 metric tonnes would only allow a 50% chance that the bluefin stocks would recover by 2023.

The proposal to ban the bluefin tuna trade at the Convention on International Trade in Endangered Species in 2010 was rejected by a number of nations, notably those most tied up in its lucrative trade. This, as well the failed attempt by the European Union Fisheries Commissioner, Maria Damanaki, to set the 2011 quota at 6,000 metric tonnes (which is now set at double that), only point to one motive for the continued over-exploitation of the bluefin tuna: financial profit.

> "€552,000 (ACTUAL SUM: US $736,000) WAS THE HIGHEST PRICE PAID FOR A SINGLE FISH AT TOKYO'S TSUKIJI FISH MARKET."

recently sold at Tokyo's Tsukiji fish market, but prices are still on the rise. This lucrative trade is bringing in profits exclusively to a small group of powerful fishing companies. The trade does not seem open to general scrutiny on the evidence of misreporting and incorrect data. Despite that, there are a total of 66 different corporations that are known to be involved in the bluefin tuna industry, as well as their having ties to Japan. Charlie Azzopardi (Azzopardi Fisheries) and Joe Caruana (Fish & Fish) are the main Maltese fish merchants and traders of all fish caught by Maltese fishermen, one of the biggest players in the industry. Similarly, other major operators include Kali Tuna D.O.O. for Croatia, Ricardo Fuentes E Hijos for Spain, Jonica Pesca S.R.I. for Italy, and Dardanel Orkinos Besiciligi Projesi for Turkey.

THE FISHING ELITE

The value of the entire trade (legal and illegal) relating to European fishermen alone is nearly €1.5 billion (US $2 billion) a year. The highest sum paid for a single fish amounted to €552,000 (actual sum: US $736,000),

> "AT THIS MOMENT EVEN AN ANNUAL QUOTA OF 8,000 METRIC TONNES WOULD ONLY ALLOW A 50% CHANCE THAT THE BLUEFIN STOCKS WOULD RECOVER BY 2023."

The most surprising Japanese company involved in the import of bluefin tuna is the car manufacturer, Mitsubishi, accounting for 40% of Mediterranean bluefin tuna imports to Japan. Others include the Sojitz Corporation (15%), Mitsui & Co., Ltd. (5%), the Maruha Corporation, the Marubeni Corporation, the Itochu Corporation and Kanetomo Co., Ltd.. The Mitsubishi Corporation is the world's largest bluefin tuna trader and is currently buying up an estimated three-quarters of the global bluefin catch every year. The fish are blast-frozen and stored in large refrigerated units, awaiting a rise in demand and scarcity of supply. As the bluefin will become increasingly endangered and prices consequently rise, Mitsubishi will be able to trade at whatever price they set. In July 2010 it stated that it will take responsibility for sourcing its bluefin tuna in a sustainable manner:

"Mitsubishi Corporation strives to preserve the global environment and pursue sustainable development through all aspects of our business." (Mitsubishi Corporation)

Any commitments to advance the situation of the bluefin tuna which also include a business agenda cannot be seen as serious support for removing the threat of bluefin extinction.

To put it mildly, the organisation responsible for managing the Atlantic bluefin tuna fishery, ICCAT, has been doing a very bad job. Catch quotas have persistently been set much higher than even their own scientific recommendations, putting huge pressure on already depleted populations of tuna. Thus, ICCAT has manifestly failed in its own aim of "maintaining the populations of tuna and tuna-like fishes at levels which will permit the maximum sustainable catch for food and other purposes." By failing in its duties as a responsible fisheries management organisation, the ICCAT is creating bigger problems, not just for itself, but for the entire Mediterranean region. Illegal, unregulated and unreported fishing is now more widespread than ever, and actual catches of bluefin have been in some cases up to five times the legal limit. This must change.

"AN INDEPENDENT STUDY OF FOUR ITALIAN PURSE SEINERS FOUND THAT EACH HAD CAUGHT OVER THREE TIMES THEIR INDIVIDUAL VESSEL QUOTAS FOR 2001."

CHAPTER SIX

TIME FOR ACTION

One thing is clear: the bluefin tuna is nearing extinction and unless we take action, the fate of the fish will continue to lie in the hands of those directly responsible for pushing it this far to the brink of extinction. Like all social change that has shaped the world we live in today, it has always been the passion of small groups and individuals that have made the desired change a reality. You can choose to be help make this change a reality, get involved, and become part of a growing movement of people who are willing to act for the oceans.

> "BECOME PART OF A GROWING MOVEMENT OF PEOPLE WHO ARE WILLING TO ACT FOR THE OCEANS."

There are various ways to get involved, make your voice heard and help to make the change that the bluefin need so badly. In this chapter we hope to inspire you to get active and help prevent this incredible species from disappearing forever.

THE BLACK FISH

This book has been published by The Black Fish, a European marine conservation organisation, which, amongst other things, takes action in defence of the bluefin tuna. We launched a direct action campaign in the Mediterranean in 2012 and intend to return to the region during future fishing seasons. As with most campaign organisations, we rely on the support of many groups, individuals and other organisations to continue our work. We are always looking for people to get involved: running their own stalls, fundraising and helping at other events, such as talks, benefit concerts and film screenings. We are also seeking people to volunteer as crew members on our vessels and become part of our direct action teams.

Whatever your skills may be, if this book has gotten your attention, get in touch with us today. Become an on-shore volunteer, supporter or activist crew member at one of the most promising and dedicated marine conservation organisations in the world. You can make a real difference for the threatened ocean wildlife.

www.theblackfish.org

POWER TO THE FORK

One of the most immediate and profound changes you can make in your own life is to stop supporting the fishing industry. As a consumer, your wallet and ultimately your fork have enormous power. Many people who become more aware of the issues surrounding industrial fishing alter their own eating habits to reflect a

"AS A CONSUMER, YOUR WALLET AND ULTIMATELY YOUR FORK HAVE ENORMOUS POWER."

more sustainable and animal-friendly lifestyle. In turn, many of them go on to inform, inspire and influence others in their own direct environment.

If you, too, have been shocked and concerned by the facts presented in this book, please consider the wider context and make the change by eliminating the consumption of all types of seafood from your diet.

The Black Fish website contains a wealth of information about European fisheries and different situations related to the current state of our oceans. There you can also find information about alternatives to seafood, fish and animal-free recipes, and how to get more active.

TAKE TO THE STREETS

If you are keen to get active, there are many different ways to get things started in your own area. Mobilise friends and others that support the cause, start a petition, make a banner and hand out leaflets outside restaurants that still sell bluefin tuna, or organise a fundraiser to enable an organisation such as The Black Fish to carry out their campaigns. The Black Fish works to support an increasing number of local campaign initiatives, so get in touch with us if you are planning something and would like some support.

EXPOSE THE RESTAURANTS

You could try to find out if any seafood restaurants in your city or town still sell bluefin tuna. If so, contact the owner, request a meeting and discuss the current situation of the bluefin tuna with them. In some cases, even people selling seafood are quite unaware of the issues and may be willing to make changes if they see potential customers are unhappy about their business practices. Politely explain why you think they should pull bluefin off their menu, while making it clear that you will not abandon your efforts until they end their sale of this endangered fish.

Unless you are successful at a first meeting, you might need to step up your campaign. You can plan to picket the restaurant, which means standing in front of it during a busy evening with banners and placards to inform visiting customers about the company selling an endangered species.

Leaflets to hand out to passers-by and people entering the premises can be downloaded or ordered through The Black Fish website.

1. Contact the owner and request a meeting.

phone   e-mail   Write

2. Go and see them.

3. Discuss current situation of Bluefin.

Another idea is to book a large part of the restaurant and then, once there, make a scene and leave, telling them you were unaware that they sold the endangered bluefin tuna and will not be associated with a restaurant which serves it. Different types of direct action tactics which cause disruption to the running of the restaurant can put pressure on the owners and have in the past shown to be an effective campaigning tool. Of course, we do not condone or encourage any illegal activity and would advise checking local legislation before any action.

MITSUBISHI

As explained earlier in this book, Mitsubishi, the car manufacturer, has its fair share in the bluefin tuna trading market, 60% of the global bluefin tuna market to be precise. Most of the fish they buy is blast-frozen and stored, awaiting demand to rise and supply to become scarce with prices rising as a consequence.

There is no doubt that the Mitsubishi Corporation has an image to uphold and would be forced to take action if multiple groups of people were to begin targeting their stores, shops and showrooms with pickets, demonstrations and other non-violent campaigns. Have a look at The Black Fish website for a full information pack on how to go about taking the campaign to a Mitsubishi outlet near you. There you will be able to find informative flyers, poster and banner designs for download or order, as well as campaign ideas.

MEET YOUR LOCAL COUNCILLOR

Some national governments as well as local councils have recently shown an interest in passing legislation to ban the sale of bluefin tuna. The more towns and cities that become bluefin tuna free, the more pressure this builds for national legislators to pass new (and hopefully effective) legislation. Monaco has taken the pioneering step to ban the sale of bluefin tuna meat, thanks largely due to the support of Prince Albert II of Monaco. Elsewhere, the Dutch Senate is already exploring ways to introduce a ban of the sale of bluefin tuna meat due to the failure of international laws to effectively stop the trade. We hope that, with sufficient support, we can work to make sure other nations follow suit. Write a letter to your local councillor and members of national and European parliaments to explain the reasons why they, too, should support the protection of the bluefin. Even better, you could try to arrange a meeting to discuss the situation face-to-face.

INVESTIGATE

If you happen to live in a region which is involved in the catching, farming or processing of bluefin tuna, it may be that you are able to assist in much-needed investigative work, providing valuable assistance to existing organisations such as The Black Fish. Please get in touch if you are able to support and collaborate with us in this way.

"SOME €20 MILLION (US $27 MILLION) OF EUROPEAN TAXPAYERS' MONEY WAS SPENT ON DEVELOPING BLUEFIN FARMS BETWEEN 1997 AND 2004."

WE ARE WORKING TO INCREASE PRESSURE ON THOSE DIRECTLY INVOLVED IN DRIVING THE BLUEFIN TUNA TO EXTINCTION TO CHANGE AND CEASE THEIR PRACTICES, AS WELL AS MAKING GOVERNMENTS FACE UP TO THEIR RESPONSIBILITY TO DEAL WITH THESE ISSUES IN AN APPROPRIATE, EFFECTIVE AND CONSISTENT MANNER.

TIME TO ACT!

It does not take a scientist to see that things are going seriously wrong in our oceans and it is in everyone's interest that we act to protect the most vulnerable of species and habitats. The work of many organisations, groups and individuals is helping to build a growing *marine conservation movement*.

Larger organisations are able to work on exposing the biggest economic culprits, such as Mitsubishi, while also engaging in direct action against the most destructive activities taking place at sea. However, the work of smaller groups and individuals plays a vital role in setting a wider change in motion: breaking open the public debate regarding fisheries and raising public awareness of the effects of their own dietary choices. This in turn works to increase pressure on those directly involved in driving the bluefin tuna to extinction to change and cease their practices, as well as forcing governments to face up to their responsibility to deal with these issues in an appropriate, effective and consistent manner.

All around us, we are witnessing a growing movement of people who are willing to stand up and take action for what is right and necessary. We hope this book has inspired you to get involved, join us and contribute your skills, enthusiasm and passion to this immense and desperate task which lies before us.

"NEVER DOUBT THAT A SMALL COMMITTED GROUP OF INDIVIDUALS CAN CHANGE THE WORLD. INDEED, IT IS THE ONLY THING THAT EVER HAS."

(MARGARET MEAD)

INDEX

ACCOBAMS **32**
albacore **31, 33, 36**
albatross **36**
almadraba **25, 73**
anchovy **23**
aquaculture **41, 44 – 47, 75**
Atlantic Ocean **22, 37**
Australia **41, 46**
blue shark **37**
body temperature **19 – 20**
breeding (see spawning)
bycatch **30, 37, 38, 73**
campaigning **12, 62, 64 – 66**
Canada **45, 46**
cetaceans **30 – 33**
CFP **53, 73**
CITES **73**
conservation organisations **33, 34, 62, 68**
consumers **42, 63**
courantille **33, 73**
Croatia **27, 30, 42, 57**

Cyprus **38**
dead zones **44**
direct action **62, 68**
disease **45, 46**
dolphins **30, 31, 33, 36, 77**
driftnet fishing **26, 30 – 37, 73, 78**
EEZ **38, 74**
endothermicity **19, 74**
enforcement **26, 38, 39, 53, 55, 56**
European Commission **35, 56, 74**
European Fisheries Fund **74**
European Union **10, 30 – 35, 41, 52, 53, 55, 56, 74, 75**
extinction **10, 15, 23, 29, 46, 56, 59, 61, 68**
feed conservation ratios **43**
feed fish **44, 46, 75**
fin whales **31, 77**
France **9, 30, 33, 53, 73, 78**
fulmars **37**
gannets **37**
Gulf of Mexico **22**
gulls **37**
habitat **17, 19, 22, 31, 36**
hake **36**
herring **44**

ICCAT **22, 27 – 29, 32, 38, 39, 50 – 56, 59, 75, 78**
illegal fishing **26, 28, 55**
industrial fishing **9, 15, 26, 49, 63, 64, 75**
Italy **29, 30, 32, 34 – 36, 57**
IWC **76**
Japan **15, 51 – 53, 57, 58, 77**
killer whales **18**
legislation **33, 34, 66**
Libya **27**
loggerhead turtle **37**
longline fishing **26, 36 – 39, 76**
mackerel **18, 44, 75**
mako sharks **18, 37**
Marine Protected Area (MPA) **76, 77**
marlins **37**
Mediterranean Sea **10, 12, 22, 23, 26 – 28, 32, 52, 55**
metabolism **19, 20, 43**
Mitsubishi **57, 58, 56**
Monaco **66**
Morocco **32, 36**
muscles **18 – 20, 42**
myoglobin **20**
Norway **46**

Oceana **34, 76, 80**
overfishing **11, 27, 28, 30, 38, 46, 55**
oxygen **19, 20, 22, 43**
pectoral fins **18**
Pelagos sanctuary **33, 77**
pilchard **46**
pilot whales **33, 77**
pineal organ **17**
politics **12, 50, 51**
pollution **44**
prey **18, 23**
Prince Albert II of Monaco **66**
purse seine fishing **26 – 30, 39, 41, 42, 52, 77**
quotas **27 – 30, 33, 34, 41, 44, 49, 51 – 53, 55 – 57, 59, 77**
refrigeration **58**
sailfish **10, 18**
salmon **18, 44 – 47**
sardines **26, 44, 46**
Sardinia **33, 77**
Scotland **46**
SCRS **53, 78**
sea birds **36, 37**
sea food alternatives **64**
sea lice **45**

sharks **17 – 19, 22, 31 – 33, 36, 37**
shearwater **36, 37**
southern bluefin tuna **41**
Spain **41, 57, 76**
spawning **22 – 23, 28, 42, 78**
sperm whales **33**
spotting planes **53 – 78**
squid **23, 44**
Strait of Gibraltar **25**
sushi **15, 52, 77**
swordfish **31, 33, 34, 36 – 38**
tailfin **17 – 19**
The Black Fish **12, 62, 64, 65, 73**
thonaille **33, 34, 78**
Total Allowable Catch (TAC) **41, 52, 78**
tuna farming **26, 41, 46, 78**
tuna species **17, 22, 41**
Turkey **28, 29, 32, 38, 57**
turtles **30 – 33, 36, 37**
United Nations **31, 32, 78**
whales **18, 20, 30, 31, 33**
WWF **27, 30, 37, 41, 79**

GLOSSARY

ACCOBAMS
The Agreement on the Conservation of Cetaceans of the Black Sea, Mediterranean Sea and contiguous Atlantic area.

Almadraba
Age-old fishing technique used to catch bluefin tuna, whereby a series of nets run from the coast into the sea, leading passing fish into a labyrinth of nets.

Aquaculture
Breeding and rearing fish in captivity.

Artisanal
Term usually used to describe small scale and traditional fishing.

The Black Fish
International marine conservation organisation on a mission to change attitudes towards our precious oceans and to work towards protecting the unique life within them. Using education, investigation and non-violent direct action, The Black Fish campaigns to end illegal and destructive fishing practices and safeguard a future for the plentiful species in our seas (www.theblackfish.org).

Bycatch
Accidental and usually unwanted catch of species other than those targeted in a particular fishing operation.

CFP
The Common Fisheries Policy is the fisheries policy of the European Union. It facilitates member state quotas on what they are allowed to catch as well as providing financial incentives to the fishing industry (ec.europa.eu/fisheries/cfp_en.htm).

CITES
Convention on International Trade in Endangered Species. Regulates the trade of endangered species of wild flora and fauna (www.cites.org).

Courantille
Type of driftnet traditionally used in France.

Driftnet
Type of fishing gear whereby a long net drifts from the surface of the water, approximately 30 to 50 meters down. The use of the nets is highly destructive as any passing animal is likely to get entangled in the net. The use of driftnets on the high seas has been banned by the United Nations since 1992.

EC
The European Commission is the executive body of the European Union. It is responsible for proposing legislation, implementing decisions, upholding the Union's treaties and the general day-to-day running of the Union (ec.europa.eu).

EEC
International organisation set up to strengthen economic ties between European nations. It was merged with other international institutions into the new framework of the European Union in 1993.

EEZ
Economic Exclusion Zones are zones which extend 200 miles out to sea, from a country's coast. Within these zones, countries have various rights over the use of the marine resources.

EFF
European Fisheries Fund is the EU fund which is allocated for supporting the fishing industry. It was set up in 2007 to replace the FIFG.

Endemic
Endemic species are species that are native to an area, as opposed to being alien or invasive species.

Endothermicity
The ability to regulate ones own body temperature, which bluefin tuna and various shark species possess.

EU
The European Union, is an economic and political union of countries primarily located in Europe. Made up of 27 member states, it is committed to regional integration, co-operation and economic and social development.

EU Fisheries Council
Council of European Fisheries ministers, making decisions on policy and the allocation of funds and quotas.

European Commission
The regulatory body of the European Union.

FAO
The Food and Agriculture Organization of the United Nations is an agency that leads international efforts to defeat hunger. It acts as a neutral forum where agreements and policy are negotiated. It also helps countries to modernise and improve agriculture, forestry and fisheries practices (www.fao.org).

FEAP
European Federation of Aquaculture Producers is the international organisation that is composed of the National Aquaculture Associations of European countries (http://www.feap.info/feap/).

Feed conversion ratios
The amount of feed fish needed to produce a certain body mass of farmed fish.

Feed fish
Fish given to farmed fish as feed.

Fecundity
The ability to reproduce or the reproductive rate of a population of fish.

FIFG
Financial Instrument for Fisheries Guidance, replaced by the EU Fisheries Fund (EFF) in 2007.

Fisheries
Entities engaged in the process of catching, processing and/or marketing of fish. Also refers to the places where fish are caught or the people involved and can be applied to a combination of fish and fishermen in specific regions, the latter fishing for similar species with similar gear types.

GFCM
General Fisheries Commission for the Mediterranean. International organisation in which 23 Member states along with the European Union work to "promote the development, conservation, rational management and best utilization of living marine resources, as well as the sustainable development of aquaculture in the Mediterranean, Black Sea and connecting waters." It was set up by the FAO in 1952.

Industrial fishing
Fishing whereby the catching and processing is aided by modern technology, such as the use of sonar to spot schools of fish underwater and the use of computer-controlled nets.

ICCAT
International Commission for the Conservation of Atlantic Tunas. ICCAT is the Regional Fisheries Management Organisation (RFMO), which regulates the bluefin tuna fishery as well as fisheries targeting swordfish, marlin, sailfish and fish from the mackerel family. Sometimes mockingly referred to as the International Conspiracy to Catch All Tuna (www.iccat.int).

IWC
The International Whaling Commission is an international body which was originally founded to regulate the whaling industry and oversee the conservation of whale stocks. It is currently made up of 84 member states and is tasked to oversee the signatories' compliance with the global moratorium on commercial whaling, which came into force in 1986 (www.iwcoffice.org).

Juveniles
Juvenile fish are younger fish that have not yet reached maturity.

Landing size
The minimum size of fish allowed (overall length) when 'landing' (bringing) a fish ashore.

Longline
Type of fishing gear whereby a kilometre-long fishing line has small lines with baited hooks hanging down approximately every 30 centimeters. As longlines catch wildlife indiscriminately, their use is controversial.

MPA
Marine Protected Areas are protected areas, the boundaries of which include some area of ocean. MPAs are defined as: "any area of the intertidal or sub-tidal terrain, together with its overlying water and associated flora, fauna, historical and cultural features, which has been reserved by law or other effective means to protect part or all of the enclosed environment" (http://www.wdpa-marine.org)

MSY
In fishing terms, Maximum Sustainable Yield is the largest amount that can be taken from a fish stock without adversely affecting its size. The concept of MSY is that only the individuals that would normally stock without adversely are taken, thus maintaining population levels. The use of MSY has come under heavy criticism in recent years as is not always easy to apply in practice, has been an ineffective and unreliable measure in fisheries management and has, in fact, only added to the problem of overfishing.

Oceana
Marine conservation organisation founded in 2001 following the merger of various groups, including the American Ocean Campaign and Pew Charitable Trusts. The organisation has offices in the US, Belgium, Spain, Chile and Belize (www.oceana.org).

Pelagic
Living in the open sea rather than

bottom of the sea. In fishing terms, it refers to those fishing practices which target species living in the open ocean, rather than deep sea species, or those living near the seabed, which are referred to as demersal species.

Pelagos Sanctuary
The largest marine protected area in the Mediterranean Sea, covering over 87,500 km², situated north of Sardinia and completely surrounding the island of Corsica. The sanctuary is believed to be an important feeding and breeding ground for species of cetaceans, including fin whales, sperm whales, Cuvier's beaked whales, pilot whales, striped dolphins, common dolphins, bottlenose dolphins and Risso's dolphins.

Population
A collection of inter-breeding organisms of a particular species.

Purse seine
Type of fishing gear which is the most commonly-used method to catch bluefin tuna. An entire school of fish is encircled by a net, then the animals are transferred into a transfer cage and pulled to a tuna farm by a tug boat.

Quota
Fishing quotas are amounts of fish that nations or individual fishermen are allowed to catch, as set by governments or fisheries management organisations. Quotas are a kind of regulated share of the catch, set in an effort to regulate fishing. A commonly used quota system is the Total Allowable Catch (TAC).

RFMO
A Regional Fisheries Management Organisation, sometimes referred to as a regional fisheries organisation, is an international organisation dedicated to the sustainable management of fishery resources in a particular region of international waters, or of highly migratory species.

Sushi and sashimi
An Japanese delicacy consisting of cooked rice and parcelled up with other ingredients, with seafood being one of the most common. Bluefin tuna is almost entirely consumed as sushi. Sashimi is a type of sushi whereby fish is served without vinegared rice.

School
A group of fish swimming in the same direction in a coordinated manner.

Spawning
When female fish produce and/or deposit a large amount of eggs in the water in order to reproduce. The young that hatch from these eggs are known as spawn. Aquatic animals such as amphibians and fish reproduce by spawning.

Spawning site fidelity
When fish return to the spot they were born, in order to spawn.

SCRS
Standing Committee on Research and Statistics, the scientific committee of the ICCAT responsible for analysing scientific data on the health of fish stocks in order to make recommendations on the yearly catch quotas (www.iccat.int/en/SCRS.htm).

SPAMI
Specially Protected Areas of Mediterranean Interest, as put in place under the Barcelona Convention.

Spotting planes
Aeroplane used to spot schools of tuna, which are then caught using purse seine fishing vessels. The use of spotting planes was banned by ICCAT in 2007 but the practice carries on regardless.

Stock
Fish stocks are sub-populations of a particular species of fish, for which certain factors such as growth, natural mortality and fishing are significant factors in determining population dynamics.

TAC
Total Allowable Catch is a quota system under which quotas are set by institutions such as the ICCAT or the EU to define how much of each species may be caught and each country is assigned a quota based on the total available and their traditional share of the catch.

Thonaille
Type of driftnet traditionally used in France.

Tuna farm
A facility which holds wild bluefin tuna in captivity, either in an off-shore sea cage or in a land-based tank. Tuna farms are usually used to hold wild caught tuna in sea cages, where the animals are fattened up prior to slaughter and export.

UN
The United Nations is an international organisation made up of 192 member states whose stated aims are to facilitate co-operation in international

law, security, economic development, social progress, human rights and the achievement of world peace. It was founded in 1945 and organisations such as the IWC, ICCAT, CITES and IUCN work within its framework and are partly funded by it (www.un.org).

WWF
The World Wide Fund for Nature (WWF) is an international NGO tasked with working on issues relating to conservation (www.wwf.org).

ACKNOWLEDGEMENTS

This publication would have never been possible without the tireless efforts from a dedicated team of contributors. Everyone's involvement was voluntary, ensuring 100% of the money raised from the sale of the book would go straight back into campaigning work.

First of all we would like to thank Josefin Robertsson and Wietse van der Werf for their initial research and writing. Their enthusiasm and drive are what pushed this book into being.

A very special mention goes to Rose Newell, who gave a lot of her time to the project, working tirelessly in her extensive editing of the book. Read more about her wide range of language services at:

www.lingocode.com

Illustrators Anieszka Banks, Benjamin Baldwin, Katja Dylla and Emily Wilson researched the issues and created some excellent illustrations for the book. Much of their work continues to be inspired by marine protection issues and will no doubt support further campaigns in future. See more of their work at:

www.anieszkabanks.com
www.katjula.com

We are grateful to conservation photographer Gary Stokes for allowing us the use of his images. Renowned for documenting the exploitation of the marine life, Gary actively supports a number of campaigns and helps to push for much needed change through his photography work. Check out his website at:

www.garystokesphotography.com

The marine conservation organisation Oceana kindly gave us permission to use some of their photographs. Explore their valuable work at:

eu.oceana.org

Helena Fletcher dedicated much of her spare time to design the layout and gave the book its final touch, ensuring its accessibility and appeal. Visit her online portfolio at:

www.helenamarie.co.uk

Mark of the Big Green Factory helped us to self-publish the book. We thank him for contributing his expertise and helping us with the printing and distribution of the book. The Big Green Factory website can be found at:

www.biggreenfactory.com

Further thanks go out to Douwe van der Werf for his advice and guidance and Martin Godard for supplying additional images.

We would also like to thank our proofreaders: David Otieno, Patrick Smith, Charlie Russell and Linda van de Kruijs for their much appreciated efforts and insights in the final stages before publication.

Finally, all of us involved in The Black Fish would like to thank everyone who has supported us along the way - our generous sponsors, our individual supporters and all those that share our cause - that is, the protection of our precious oceans and those who inhabit their depths.

PHOTO CREDITS

All images are copyrighted and may not be reproduced without written permission from the respective copyright holder(s). The copyright of any images not listed here lies with The Black Fish.

BENJAMIN BALDWIN
9, 10, 12, 21, 28, 46, 60

ANIESZKA BANKS
8, 13, 20, 40, 49

ANIESZKA BANKS & EMILY WILSON
25, 31, 35, 37, 38, 42, 43, 48, 54, 65, 67

KATJA DYLLA
cover, 18, 32, 63

MARTIN GODARD
27, 44, 58

OCEANA LX
16 (left), 29, 51, 57, 68

OCEANA CARLOS SUÁREZ
30

GARY STOKES
11, 12, 14, 16 (right) 17, 24, 50, 61